Leader's Guide

The Love, Sex, and Dating Series

Other titles available in the Love, Sex, and Dating series
by Barry St. Clair and Bill Jones:
  LOVE: Making It Last
  SEX: Desiring the Best
  DATING: Going Out in Style

Also available by Barry and Carol St. Clair
  Talking with Your Kids about Love, Sex, and Dating

Leader's Guide

The Love, Sex, and Dating Series

Tim Atkins, Vince Morris & Gene DiPaolo

VICTOR BOOKS

A DIVISION OF SCRIPTURE PRESS PUBLICATIONS INC.
USA CANADA ENGLAND

Unless otherwise indicated, Scripture taken from the HOLY BIBLE, NEW INTERNATIONAL
VERSION. Copyright © 1973, 1978, 1984 by International Bible Society. Used by permis-
sion of Zondervan Publishing House. All rights reserved.

Scripture quotations designated NASB are from *The New American Standard Bible,*
© The Lockman Foundation 1960, 1962, 1963, 1968, 1971, 1972, 1975, 1977.

ISBN 1-56476-237-8

Cover Design: Joe DeLeon

Produced for Victor Books by the Livingstone Corporation. David R. Veerman,
J. Michael Kendrick, and Brenda James Todd, project staff.
Printed in the United States of America

Contents

Contents

About the Authors

TIM ATKINS is currently youth pastor at Faith Baptist Church in Fort Wayne, Indiana. He holds a B.A. in Christian education from Huntington College and has 16 years' experience as a youth worker. Tim has contributed to several books, including Flex Sessions (Victor Books) and *Video Movies Worth Watching* (Baker). He and his wife Patty have three children.

GENE DI PAOLO is presently completing his law studies at the University of North Carolina at Chapel Hill, where he is managing director of the North Carolina Lawyers' Research Service. He holds degrees from the University of Akron and Dallas Theological Seminary and has been a pastor of student ministries. Gene has contributed to *Youthwalk*, *Video Movies Worth Watching* (Baker), and *LessonSearch* and *LessonMaker* (NavPress).

VINCE MORRIS has been the youth minister at Immanuel Presbyterian Church in Warrenville, Illinois since October 1989. He has a B.A. in youth ministry from Gordon College and has organized missions trips to inner-city Chicago, rural Appalachia, and Guatemala. Vince and his wife Ellen live in Wheaton, Illinois.

How to Use the Leader's Guide

This leader's guide is designed to supplement the books in Barry St. Clair and Bill Jones's Love, Sex, and Dating series. It is flexible tool that will help your students get the most out the books they'll be reading.

Each lesson has the following features:

Objective: a concise summary of what your students will learn in the lesson

Bible Passages: a list of the Scripture readings used in the Study section

Materials Checklist: a review of the items you'll need for the meeting

Starter: a fun activity designed to introduce the evening's topic to the group

Study: a series of interactive questions that get students thinking about the important ideas in the book

Application: an activity that is meant to encourage students to apply what they've learned to their lives

Optional Activity: an additional game or event for more active groups with larger blocks of time available

In this leader's guide are two approaches for covering the books in the Love, Sex, and Dating series. If you have very limited time for discussing these books, you may be inclined to choose the first option. It allows you to cover an entire book in one lesson. Have your students read the entire book or key chapters of the book before the meeting. Then find the "overview in one lesson" in this guide that corresponds to that book. The lesson emphasizes highlights of the book and allows students to absorb key ideas.

If you intend to go through the books in a more detailed, systematic way, you should choose the second option, which provides four lessons for each book. Each lesson corresponds with three chapters in the book; lesson 1 goes with chapters 1-3, lesson 2 with chapters 4-6, and so on. The lessons build on ideas that are discussed in previous lessons, but they can also stand alone.

You should not hesitate to adapt lessons to the needs of your group. In particular, we encourage you to add or adjust study questions to help your young people with specific concerns they may have about love, sex, and dating. We hope this leader's guide gives you valuable insights for guiding your group through these important issues.

Part 1

LESSONS FOR
Love: Making It Last

TIM ATKINS

Making It Last

An Overview in One Lesson

Objective	As a result of this study, students will learn the true basis for a loving relationship that leads to marriage.
Bible Passages	Various passages.
Materials Checklist	☐ notebook paper ☐ pens/pencils ☐ large sketch pad or chalkboard ☐ handout with Bible verses (see Study)
Starter (20 minutes)	**The Perfect Mate** Divide your group into male and female. The guys will be creating the perfect girl, while the girls will be creating the perfect guy. Give each group a list of features, as well as paper and pencils. They are to name a famous person for each feature. For example, the ideal guy may have the body of Sylvester Stallone, the eyes of Mel Gibson, and the height of Michael Jordan. After the two groups present their ideal person, ask: **In what ways do we use these models to set our standards in our search for the ideal mate? What's wrong with using these standards?**

Features:

Eyes	Voice	Skin
Mouth	Mind	Family
Hair	Height	Teeth
Body	Clothes	Feet
Hands	Humor	Personality

Study
(15 minutes)

On a large sheet of paper (or on a chalkboard) draw a horizontal time line. At the left end, write "Just met." At the right end, write "Marriage." At various points along the line, write the following: "Good Friends," "Begin Dating," "Going Steady," "Conflicts," "Declaration of Love," and "Proposal." Next, pass out a handout with the verses below. Have a group member look up and read each verse aloud. The group must then decide at what point on the time line that verse should be considered. Write the Scripture reference and a one or two word description at that point on the line.

1 Timothy 1:15	Proverbs 27:9
1 John 4:7-11	Proverbs 18:24
Proverbs 27:4	Psalm 139:23-24
Ephesians 4:15	James 3:16
Philippians 2:4	2 Corinthians 6:14
Colossians 3:15	Colossians 4:6

Application
(15 minutes)

Have your group read 1 Corinthians 13 silently. Use a chalkboard or overhead projector to write down their responses as they list the characteristics of love found in this chapter. Examine each characteristic one at a time. Have the group members identify situations in their own lives that reflect how we fail at this type of love. For example, under "love is kind," they might say, "I cut down my girlfriend in front of my friends." Then have the group give suggestions of not only how to solve the failures mentioned, but also how to demonstrate the characteristic the Bible is talking about. Encourage your group to be specific in discussing failures and to be creative in finding solutions. This is your chance to take a biblical passage and give it real meaning in their daily lives.

Optional Activity

Stage a large group date. Arrange the group to do an activity together. After everyone arrives for the activity, explain that on this date everyone will be reversing roles. Pair the group off randomly into couples. Start by requiring the girl to ask the guy to go out with her. Throughout your activity, remind them of their role reversals. Girls should hold doors for the guys, offer to get soft drinks or food, and so on. Guys should let the girls help them out in any way they can.

After the activity, plan to have some time to discuss the event. Ask how they felt about switching roles. Discuss what aspects of dating are difficult and which ones are worth the effort. Remind the group that almost without exception their marriage relationship will begin in a dating relationship. When you learn to begin that relationship in Christ and follow through, your marriage will truly be a gift from God.

One

Discovering the Real Thing

Objective	As a result of this study, students will be able to determine which of their views on love and relationships are based on fantasy and which ones are rooted in reality.
Bible Passage	1 Corinthians 13:1-13
Materials Checklist	☐ pencils/pens ☐ sheets of paper ☐ list of ideal characteristics (see Starter) ☐ video camera (optional) ☐ recording of Michael W. Smith song "Picture Perfect" (optional)
Starter (20 minutes)	**The Perfect Mate** Divide your group into male and female. The guys will be creating the perfect girl, while the girls will be creating the perfect guy. Give each group a list of features, as well as paper and pencils. They are to name a famous person for each feature. For example, the ideal guy may have the body of Sylvester Stallone, the eyes of Mel Gibson, and the height of Michael Jordan. After the two groups present their ideal person, ask: **In what ways do we use these models to**

set our standards in our search for the ideal mate? What's wrong with using these standards?

Features:

Eyes	Voice	Skin
Mouth	Mind	Family
Hair	Height	Teeth
Body	Clothes	Feet
Hands	Humor	Personality

Study
(15 minutes)

Say: **We've talked about the standards we use in searching for the right one. Now let's dig a little deeper and look at some common ideas—and misconceptions—that many people have about love. Then we'll study what God has to say about those ideas.**

During this time, your group will try to identify concepts about love that are myths and concepts that are true. Designate one side of the room as "truth" and one side as "myth." Read the statements below one at a time. As you read a statement, have the group members move to the side of the room they feel fits the statement. If they believe the statement is true, they will move to the "truth" side, if it is a myth, they will move to the other side. Pause after each question and ask a representative from each side to give reasons to support their group's belief.

1. My feelings will tell me when I have found true love. (False—See p. 13 of *Love: Making It Last*.)

2. Love can occur at first sight. (False—See p. 16.)

3. People who have real love experience little conflict or tension. (False—See pp. 16–17.)

4. If you keep the person you date from being with his or her friends, it is probably a sign of jealousy. (True—See pp. 34–35.)

5. A genuine love relationship can begin with infatuation. (True—See pp. 17.)

18

6. In real love, the feelings last a lifetime. (False—See p. 13.)

7. A person who loves another person no matter what his or her looks or personality is probably showing true love. (True—see p. 26–27.)

8. People who know real love have an idealized image of their partner. (False—See p. 18.)

After you have read these statements, reveal which ones are myths and which ones are true. Then ask the following questions:

1. Which of the myths in the statements just read did you fall for?

2. Why does God want us to discover true love in our relationships?

3. What tests would you apply to discover if you were in love?

Application
(15 minutes)

Have your group read 1 Corinthians 13 silently. Use a chalkboard or overhead projector to write down their responses as they list the characteristics of love found in this chapter. Examine each characteristic one at a time. Have the group members identify situations in their own lives that reflect how we fail at this type of love. For example, under "love is kind," they might say, "I cut down my girlfriend in front of my friends." Then have the group give suggestions of not only how to solve the failures mentioned, but also how to demonstrate the characteristic the Bible is talking about. Encourage your group to be specific in discussing failures and to be creative in finding solutions. This is your chance to take a biblical passage and give it real meaning in their daily lives.

Optional Activity

Divide your group into two smaller groups. Have each group write a "script" for a series of actions to go along with Michael W. Smith's song "Picture Perfect." Using a video camera, tape each group's creative interpretation of this song

19

while the music plays. Afterward, play back the results for the entire group. You may want to serve popcorn while they watch.

Two
Building Relationships

Objective	As a result of this study, students will identify skills needed to develop lasting relationships and to move these relationships to a deeper level.
Bible Passage	Philippians 2:1-4
Materials Checklist	☐ notebook paper ☐ pens/pencils ☐ Friendship goal sheet (see Application)
Starter (20 minutes)	**False Impressions** This starter will help your group members realize they don't know each other as well as they thought. Divide the group into small groups. Have each person jot down four statements about himself or herself. One statement will be a lie and the other three will be true. (Encourage group members to come up with true statements that are bizarre or unusual to add to the mystery.) Example: 1. "I once owned a pet snake." (T) 2. "I have been bungee jumping twice in the past year." (F)

3. "I am related to former president Jimmy Carter." (T)

4. "I lived in Japan for a year." (T)

One at a time, have group members read their statements. The group will try to identify which statement is false.

Study
(15 minutes)

Say: **We just found out that we often don't know as much about people as we thought we did. True friendships involve a lot more than superficial conversations and occasional get-togethers. Let's see how we can build strong friendships that form the foundation for possible love relationships.**

Have the group read silently Philippians 2:1-4. Encourage a couple of people in the group to paraphrase this passage so that it talks specifically about how to treat friends. Tell them to keep this in mind as they do the next exercise.

For this activity, you will need to divide the group into pairs. You are going to identify for them five levels of communication that we use on a daily basis. (John Powell's book *Why Am I Afraid to Tell You Who I Am?* gives a complete explanation of these levels of conversation. First, name and define each level. Read the examples provided. Next explain to the group that partners are to answer the question "How was your day?" for each level of conversation described. You may need to repeat the descriptions of the different levels as partners continue the exercise.

Level 5: Cliché Conversation

This is the most shallow level of communication. It includes those things we say over and over without really giving information, such as "Have a nice day" or "How's it going?"

Level 4: Reporting the Facts

At this level, you give information that is public knowledge: "The store is open seven days

22

a week" or "She visited her sister yesterday."

Level 3: Voicing Ideas and Judgments

At this level, you begin to share personal information. "Math is hard for me." "I don't think he should have taken his dad's car."

Level 2: Expressing Feelings

When you share real emotions, you are sharing at level 2. "I feel left out." "I'm jealous."

Level 1: Transparency

This is the deepest level of communication. "I think I love you." "I'm really hurting."

After the partners have had a chance to answer "How was your day?" at all five levels, discuss their reactions. Have the group identify which level is most comfortable. Discuss why levels 1 and 2 are difficult. Finally, decide at what level Philippians 2:1-4 is directing us to communicate.

Application
(15 minutes)

The following are five elements to a successful friendship as outlined by Alan McGinnis in *The Friendship Factor*. Discuss each element with the group and then hand out the friendship goal sheet. Have the students identify one friend and then write action steps under each element that they will use to improve their friendships.

FRIENDSHIP GOAL SHEET

1. **Make friendship a priority.** Your friendships require time and energy. Like anything else at which you wish to excel, you must put forth effort in order to develop real friends.

2. **Learn the gestures of love.** You need to determine what actions express loving and caring for your friend. For one friend, it might be sending her a card in the mail. For another, it might entail coming to watch him play at his sport. Gestures are different for different

people.

3. **Create space.** Every friendship, every relationship needs time away from the relationship. Time needs to be spent away from each other developing individual characteristics and developing other relationships.

4. **Dare to talk about your affections.** You must learn to say what you feel. Whether verbal or written, let your friend know exactly what it is that makes you glad to have him or her for a friend.

5. **Be transparent.** True friends are able to move to the deepest level of communication. They are open and honest and willing to share what is real for them.

Conclude by saying something like: **By now we should realize that true love begins with friendship—the kind of friendship that is self-sacrificing, always eager to look out for that person's good. During the coming week, I encourage you to think about ways you can be a better friend to everyone you know.**

Optional Activities

1. Throw a Q & A party. Serve snacks and spend the entire time answering questions at random from *Talk Triggers* by Thom and Joanie Schultz (Group Publishers). You also could have the students write their own questions. Make a list of 50 or so and then spend the rest of the time answering those.

2. Have each student choose the things from the serving list on pages 76–78 of *Love: Making It Last*. Give them a week to complete the tasks. At your next meeting, have your students discuss how they felt while serving and how their friends reacted to their actions.

24

Three

Resolving Conflicts

Objective | As a result of this study, students will identify common conflicts and tensions found in relationships and will learn how to resolve them in a godly way.

Bible Passages | Hebrews 12:5-13 and other verses.

Materials Checklist |
☐ notebook paper
☐ pencils/pens
☐ 3 x 5 cards (optional)

Starter
(20 minutes)

Dear John Letter

Divide your group into smaller groups. Give one person in each group a piece of paper with the words "Dear John" written at the top of the letter. Everyone in the group is to contribute one sentence to a breakup letter that "John" will receive from the girlfriend who is about to dump him. (Allow 5-10 minutes for this part.) Afterward, collect the letters and read them to your group. Then ask: **If someone were writing this letter to you, how would you want it to be different from the one John received?** Ask group members to share any experiences they have had with "Dear John" letters.

Study

Have the group brainstorm a list of conflicts and tensions that often occur in relationships. Some examples would be cheating on each other, pressures to get physical, dislike of the boy-friend's/girlfriend's friends. For each conflict, list what a typical response would be. Then set the list aside.

Use the verses listed below to explore godly ways to handle conflicts. Read each verse aloud. Have the group determine what each verse says to do when faced with conflicts.

2 Corinthians 1:8-10

2 Corinthians 4:7-18

Philippians 1:12-14

Hebrews 12:5-13

James 1:2-4

After all the passages have been studied, go back to your list of relationship conflicts. Using the information from the verses, discuss ways to resolve the conflicts from a biblical standpoint. Encourage your group to be realistic and specific.

Application

(15 minutes)

Have your group members lay on the floor and close their eyes. (If this is not possible, have them get as comfortable as possible and close their eyes). Instruct them to think of a conflict that they have experienced in a relationship. It may be one that they are facing now or one that has happened in the past. Ask them to imagine that the person is standing before them right now. Explain that they are going to resolve that conflict in their imagination, using the lessons learned from the Scriptures and these "Rules of the Ring" of *Love: Making It Last* (p. 86). Read each rule and then pause, allowing your group to take that rule and play it out in the scene in their heads.

1. Become more sensitive to your friend.

2. Try to understand your friend better.

3. Be spiritually mature.

4. Choose the right timing.

5. Desire openness.

6. Stop everything else.

7. Select the right words.

8. Guard your tone of voice.

9. Talk out your feelings.

10. Look at the other person's point of view.

11. Identify the problem.

12. Determine the solution.

13. Accept any correction.

14. Confess any wrongdoing.

15. Forgive any wrongdoing.

16. Pray together.

17. Deal with the little issues.

Conclude by saying: **Conflicts are inevitable in any relationship. The way you handle conflicts will determine whether that relationship will grow or die. Decide right now to bring all your conflicts before God. Avoid "fighting dirty" and honor Christ by treating the other person with love and respect.**

Optional Activity

Pass out 3 x 5 cards to each group member. Instruct them to write on the card the name of a person with whom they are experiencing conflicts or a brief description of a conflict they are struggling with. Encourage them to leave out identifying information. Their card may simply have a name on it, or it may be something like "pressure to party." Put all the cards in a pile in the middle. Next, have each person take a card other than their own. Group members should pray for the person/conflict on their new card.

NOTES

You could have a large group prayer, going around the circle with each person praying a brief prayer for the problem listed on the card, or you may want to break into smaller groups to pray.

Four

Finding the Right One

Objective	As a result of this study, students will learn ways to identify relationships that will last.
Bible Passages	Song of Solomon 8:6-7 and other verses.
Materials Checklist	☐ notebook paper ☐ pens/pencils
Starters (20 minutes)	**Take My Wife, Please** Give the names of these real-life people and fictitious characters below, and have the group identify each spouse.

1. Barney Rubble of "The Flintstones"
   (Betty)
2. Howard Cunningham of "Happy Days"
   (Marian)
3. Homer Simpson of "The Simpsons"
   (Marge)
4. Steven Keaton of "Family Ties"
   (Elyce)
5. Bill Clinton
   (Hillary)
6. Ricky Ricardo
   (Lucy)
7. Tim Taylor of "Home Improvement"
   (Jill)

8. Ward Cleaver of "Leave it to Beaver"
   (June)

9. Bruce Willis
   (Demi Moore)

10. Tom Cruise
    (Nicole Kidman)

11. David Bowie
    (Iman)

12. Billy Joel
    (Christie Brinkley)

13. George Bailey of *It's a Wonderful Life*
    (Mary)

14. Elvis Presley
    (Priscilla)

15. Rocky Balboa of *Rocky*
    (Adrian)

Mating Rating

Use this starter to move the group toward the idea of their own future mate. Divide the group into guys and girls. Give each group a piece of paper. Tell them to write down characteristics they want the person they marry to have. Compare the two lists. Ask: **In what ways are your lists similar? Are they realistic? Are they spiritual?**

Study
(15 minutes)

Because it is likely that few, if any, young people in your group are currently in relationships that will culminate in marriage, this study will focus on identifying positive and negative aspects of marriage relationships detailed in the Bible. As your group studies the passages, you will want to tell them to disregard the unusual customs (such as concubines and polygamy) and concentrate on finding the lesson of the story. As you discuss each story, try to come up with an overall lesson to be learned.

In summarizing this section, point out how different each of these relationships were. Every relationship has a different process, different circumstances, and different responses. You should stress, however, that all true, right relationships are God-centered. Discuss the lessons from the passages, then have group members draw applications that they can remember for their own lives.

Here are some examples:

Passage	Main idea	Application
Song of Solomon 8:6-7	Love is permanent and valuable.	The love for my future spouse must be placed above myself and my possessions.
1 Kings 11:1-13	King Solomon's wives turned him away from God.	I should choose a godly wife who will help me in my spiritual walk.
2 Samuel 11:1-27; 2 Samuel 12:1-14	King David took what he wanted without God's leading and at the expense of others.	When I shut God out of my relationships, I can expect sorrow and pain.
Genesis 24:1-16, 61-67	Abraham's servant prayed for God's guidance.	I must trust God to provide the right person for me.
Genesis 29:14-30	Jacob was patient and worked for the right mate.	The right mate is worth working and waiting for.

Application

(15 minutes)

Give each group member a piece of paper and a pen or pencil. On one side of the paper have them write at the top *I, (name), wish for my wife/husband to have the following qualities:* Underneath it, they should write qualities, characteristics or actions they wish to see in their future spouses. These may be things ranging from a sense of humor to physical purity to a commitment to God. After they have finished this, have them turn the paper over and write at the top *I, (name), promise my future wife/husband to have the following:* Under this heading, they should write qualities, characteristics, and actions they will bring to their marriage. When everyone has finished, have them put their paper in an envelope, seal it, and address it to their future spouse. Encourage them to keep this in a place to use at a later time.

Optional Activity

Invite several married couples to serve as a panel. Try to have representatives from different age groups and couples who had variety of dating experiences that led up to their marriage. Let your group ask them questions. If your group is hesitant, have ready a list of questions for the panel. Below is a list you might use:

1. How old were you when you first met?

2. How long did you date?

3. How much time passed before you said "I love you"?

4. Who said "I love you" first?

5. How long were you engaged?

6. What was the most romantic thing he/she did for you?

7. When was your first fight?

8. What was it about?

9. What made you decide to marry this person?

10. What is the hardest thing about marriage?

Part 2

LESSONS FOR
Sex: Desiring the Best

GENE DiPAOLO

Desiring the Best

An Overview in One Lesson

Objective	As a result of this study, students should understand that sex is good; that God wants them to wait until marriage to have sex; and how to get control over their sex lives so that they can follow God's plan.
Bible Passages	Genesis 1:26-28, 31; 1 Thessalonians 4:3-6
Materials Checklist	☐ pencils/pens ☐ pads of note paper ☐ letter-size envelopes ☐ 3 x 5 index cards ☐ 86 one-inch squares of paper (optional) ☐ 86 small balloons
Starter (20 minutes)	**Top Ten Lists** Have someone read aloud the parable "The Golden Locket" that appears in *Sex: Desiring the Best*. Ask another person from the group to summarize the point of the parable. (Possible answers: If you have sex before marriage, it won't be as special when you get married. Sex before marriage diminishes its enjoyment in marriage.) Ask the rest of the group to respond

35

to the summary. Did it express the main point of the parable? If appropriate, ask others to offer their summary of the parable. Get similar feedback from the group.

Divide the group into two teams. Provide each team with a pencil and a pad of paper. For each team, appoint a team leader to generate discussion and a team secretary to take notes. Have one team come up with a list of the top ten reasons, listed in reverse chronological order (beginning with number 10) why someone should wait until marriage to have sex. (Examples: God's way is the best way. Abstinence is the only way to avoid teen pregnancy.) Have the other team come up with a list of the top ten reasons, also listed in reverse chronological order, why someone *shouldn't* wait until marriage to have sex (Examples: It's the only way to really express your feelings for another person. You can avoid all the negative consequences of premarital sex by using contraceptives.)

After each group has been given sufficient time to come up with their list of ten reasons (5-10 minutes), have everyone rejoin the larger group. Have each group's secretary report their list, in reverse chronological order. Write each team's list on an overhead or chalkboard. Have the group select the most persuasive reason from each list. Have them share why they think these reasons are so persuasive.

Study
(15 minutes)

Say: **Let's take a few minutes to talk about what God has to say about sex. Lets see why He wants you to wait until marriage to have sex and how you can get control over your sex life so that you can wait.**

Note: The following study contains lesson overviews from chapters 1, 4, and 12. Each overview is accompanied by some discussion questions.

1. Ask: **Why do some people think sex i**

NOTES

dirty? Have a group member read Genesis 1:26-28, 31 and Genesis 2:18-24. Then ask: **From what these passages tell you, why did God create sex?**

Review the fact that God designed sex for four main reasons: (1) to make babies; (2) to enjoy pleasure; (3) to express love; and, most importantly, (4) to join personalities ("becoming one flesh"). Share that God planned for sex to be enjoyed in the context of marriage. Point out that since God is the creator of sex, it only makes sense that people should follow his plan—in the Bible—for its use.

2. Have someone read aloud 1 Thessalonians 4:3-6. Ask: **What do you think that the apostle Paul meant when he used the term "sexual immorality" in this passage? How does this passage apply to our own sexual behavior?**

Point out that the term means more than "sexual intercourse." It means something like "messing around with sex." What Paul is teaching is that we should learn to control our body when it comes to any kind of physical contact that is related to sex—from holding hands, to kissing, to touching body parts.

3. What is the best way for a person to gain control over his or her sexual behavior? What should a person do if he or she has messed up in this area? What steps does a person need to take to stay out of trouble?

Most people in your group will fall into one of two categories: (1) those who have messed-up sex lives they need to get under control; and (2) those who haven't gotten into trouble yet, but don't have a plan for keeping out of trouble. The first group needs a plan to get control, the second group needs a plan so they don't lose control. Share the book's four steps to gaining control: (1) realizing the need for control; (2) deciding to flee evil desires; (3) focusing on your relationship with Christ; and (4) making friends who have similar convictions.

Application
(15 minutes)

Ask the following question: **What important truths did you learn from the lesson?** (e.g., Sex is good; God wants people to wait until marriage to have sex; reasons for gaining control over sexual desires). Make a list of their answers on the overhead or chalkboard. Make sure their answers cover most of the main points from the study. When the list is complete, ask: **How should the truths we've listed affect your lives?** (Possible answers: We should wait until marriage to have sex. We need to get control over our sexual desires before they get control of us.)

Next, divide students into small groups. Tell each group to write a television public service announcement that promotes the idea of waiting until marriage to have sex. Group members may either read their scripts or act them out. Have the groups vote on the best announcement.

Optional Activity

Supplies: You will need 86 small one-inch square pieces of paper and 86 balloons.

Before the meeting: Write one letter from the following phrases on each square of paper: Sex is good because God made it; Sex is worth waiting for; God's plan for sex is best; The only safe sex is no sex. Put one piece of paper with a letter written on it into each balloon. Blow up the balloons. Put all the balloons in a big plastic trash bag.

At the meeting: Divide the group into four smaller groups. Say something like: **Inside each balloon is a small piece of paper with a letter written on it. There are enough letters to spell the following phrases** (write the phrases on the overhead or board). **When I toss out the the balloons, you should pop them**

NOTES

to get the letters out. The first team to spell one of the key phrases wins a prize. (It can be anything you choose.) Also, to avoid a chaotic situation, you may want to have one representative from each team pop a balloon, return to his or her team with the letter, then send another representative to get the next letter. To prevent a deadlock, you may allow teams to swap letters.

Open the top of the plastic bag. Swing the bag from the bottom so that all the balloons fly out at once, and watch the fun begin.

One

Understanding Sex

Objective	As a result of this study, students should understand that sex is good and that following God's plan for sex will protect relationships from unhappy consequences.
Bible Passages	Genesis 1:26-28, 31; 2:18-24
Materials Checklist	☐ pads of paper ☐ pencils or pens ☐ index cards ☐ standard size envelopes ☐ 45 one-inch squares of paper (optional) ☐ 45 balloons (optional)
Starter (20 minutes)	**Surrounded by Sex** Divide your group into two smaller groups. Supply each group with a pencil and pad of paper. Designate a leader in each group to generate discussion and a person to take notes. This person should be instructed to write down the group's findings so that he or she can report when the large group gets back together. Have the first group brainstorm to come up with as many songs as they can that say some-

41

thing about sex either in their title or in their lyrics ("I Want Your Sex," "Like a Virgin," and so on). Have the second group brainstorm to think of television commercials that use sex to sell their products.

After each group has had sufficient time to talk over their ideas (5-10 minutes), have everyone rejoin the large group. One by one, have each group give a verbal report of their findings. Make a list of each group's comments on an overhead or blackboard.

Take the remaining time to discuss each group's findings. For each song, have the group complete the following sentence: "This song says sex is (fun, natural, okay when you're in love, and so on). Ask: **Do you think what these songs say about sex is true? Why or why not?**

For the commercials, ask the group why advertisers use sex to sell their products. Then ask **What is so deceptive about this approach to selling products? What false ideas about sex are shown in commercials?** Give everyone a chance to respond.

Study
(15 minutes)

Say: **We've seen what our society is telling us about sex. Now let's study what God has to say about this important subject.**

1. Ask: **Why do some people think sex is dirty?** Have a group member read aloud Genesis 1:26-28, 31 and Genesis 2:18-24. Then ask **From what these passages tell you, why did God create sex?**

Review the fact that God designed sex for four main reasons: (1) to make babies; (2) to enjoy pleasure; (3) to express love; and, most importantly, (4) to join personalities ("becoming one flesh"). Share that God planned for sex to be enjoyed in the context of marriage. Point out that since God is the creator of sex, it only makes sense that people should follow his plan—in the

42

Bible—for its use.

2. Ask: **When have you thought that members of the opposite sex were weird or strange? What are the significant differences between men and women?** Highlight the differences between guys and girls stressed in chapters 2 and 3 of the book. In their spirit guys are tough, while girls are tender. Guys tend to be turned on by looks and are easily physically aroused. Girls, on the other hand, respond to romance and take more time to become sexually aroused.

3. Ask: **What is the toughest or worst thing about being a guy? What is the toughest or worst thing about being a girl? How can our relationship with Christ help us out with these problems?**

Young men and women need to take the time to learn about the nature and needs of the opposite sex. Point out that girls should understand the tremendous sexual struggle that guys face. Encourage them to help with this struggle by doing their best to keep the physical relationship to a minimum. Guys need to recognize the deep desire girls have for a sense of security. They should be encouraged to concentrate on girl's spiritual and emotional needs and to do all they can to help her meet these needs.

Application
(15 minutes)

Say something like: **We have covered a lot a material. I want to give you an opportunity to respond to what you have learned.**

Ask: **What important truths did you learn from this study?** (Possible answers: God made guys and girls different; sex is not dirty; and so on.) Make a list of their answers on the overhead or chalkboard. Make sure their answers cover the main points from the study. When the list is complete, ask the following question: **How should what we've studied impact your behavior?** (Example: We should take time to learn about the needs and struggles of the opposite sex.)

Provide each student with a pencil, an index card, and an envelope. Have them write one thing that they learned from this lesson on the front of the card (I learned that guys are turned on by looks). Then have them write what they plan to do with this knowledge on the back of the card. An example might be "I will dress modestly when I go out with a guy so that I don't turn him on sexually." Have them take the cards home, and encourage them to keep the cards in a place where they'll be reminded of their plans.

Optional Activity

Balloon Scramble

You'll need 45 one-inch squares of paper and 45 balloons for this exercise. Before the meeting, write one letter from the following four phrases on each piece of paper: sex is good; God made sex; guys are tough; girls are tender. (In other words, write *s* on the first piece of paper, *e* on the second, *x* on the third, and so on.) Put one piece of paper with a letter written on it into each balloon. Blow up the balloons. Put all the balloons in a big plastic trash bag. Also, write the phrases on a chalkboard, large sheet of paper, or overhead projector.

At the meeting, divide the group into four smaller groups. Say something like: **Inside each balloon is a small piece of paper with a letter written on it. There are enough letters to spell four key phrases from our lesson. When I toss out the balloons, you should pop them to get the letters out. The first team to spell a key phrase from our lesson wins.** (Purchase an appropriate prize before the meeting.) Also, to avoid a chaotic situation, you may want to have one representative from each team pop a balloon, return to his or her team with the letter, then send another representative to get the next letter. To

NOTES

prevent a deadlock, you may allow teams to swap letters.

Open the top of the plastic bag. Swing the bag from the bottom so that all the balloons fly out at once, and watch the fun begin.

Two

Waiting Is Important

Objective	As a result of this lesson, students should understand why God wants them to wait until marriage to have sex and how they should obey God's wisdom for keeping physical contact to a minimum.
Bible Passage	1 Thessalonians 4:3-6
Materials Checklist	☐ pads of paper ☐ pens and pencils
Starter (20 minutes)	**Top Ten Lists** Have someone read aloud the parable "The Golden Locket" that appears at the beginning of *Sex: Desiring the Best*. Ask someone from the group to summarize the point of the parable. (Examples: "If you have sex before marriage, it won't be as special when you get married" or "Sex before marriage reduces its enjoyment in marriage.") Have the rest of the group respond to this summary. Ask: **Did it express the main point of the parable?** If time allows, ask others to offer their summary of the parable. Divide the group into two teams. Provide each team with a pencil and a pad of paper. For each team, appoint a team leader to generate

discussion and a team secretary to take notes. Have one team come up with a list of the top ten reasons, listed in reverse chronological order (that is, beginning with number 10) why someone should wait until marriage to have sex. ("God's way is the best way" or "It's the only way to avoid teen pregnancy" are two examples.) Have the other team come up with a list of the top ten reasons, also listed in reverse chronological order, why someone shouldn't wait until marriage to have sex. (Examples would include statements like "It's the only way to really express your feelings for another person" or "It doesn't really hurt anybody.")

After each group has been given sufficient time to come up with their list of ten reasons (5-10 minutes), have everyone rejoin the larger group. Have each group's secretary report his or her team's list, in reverse chronological order. Write each team's list on an overhead or chalkboard. Have the group select the reason from each list that they think is the most persuasive. Have them share why they think the selected reasons are so appealing.

Study
(15 minutes)

Say something like: **We've looked at the reasons why someone should wait to have sex and the reasons why someone shouldn't wait to have sex. Let's take a few minutes to talk about why God wants you to wait until marriage to have sex and how you can follow that plan.**

Go over the following questions with your group:

1. What makes waiting until marriage to have sex so difficult? Is waiting tougher for guys or girls? Have them explain their answers.

Make the point that it is worth waiting until marriage to have sex because that is how God designed sex to be experienced. It only makes sense that if God created sex to be enjoyed in a certain way that anything else would be less than the best. In order to enjoy sex later and have the best marriage possible, it is necessary to say no to sex now.

2. Have someone read 1 Thessalonians 4:3-6. Ask: **What do you think that the apostle Paul meant when he used the term "sexual immorality" in this passage? How does this passage apply to our own sexual behavior?**

Point out that the term means more than "sexual intercourse." It means something like "messing around with sex." What Paul is teaching is that we should learn to control our body when it comes to any kind of physical contact that is related to sex—from holding hands, to kissing, to touching body parts.

3. From whom or what do young people feel the most pressure to engage in sex (friends, T.V., movies, and so on)?

According to *Sex: Desiring the Best*, pressure to have sex comes from four areas: (1) a desire to get revenge against parents; (2) a need to feel popular; (3) longing for acceptance; and (4) a need for security. Point out that premarital sex will not provide lasting popularity, true acceptance, or real security. Stress the need to resist temptation in the manner outlined in James 1.

Application
(15 minutes)

Provide each member of the group with a few sheets of notebook paper and a pencil. Have each student write a one- or two-page letter to someone who has asked the following questions:

(1) Why you think a person should wait until marriage to have sex?

(2) What limits or guidelines have you set or will you set for yourself in terms of what you will and will not do on a date?

(3) How have you or how will you deal with pressure to have sex from your boyfriend, girl-

friend, friends, or anyone else?

Ask for volunteers from the group to share one of their answers with the rest of the group. Ideally, you will want at least one person to share his or her answer for each question. If time permits, you may want to have more than one person share his or her answer for each question.

If members of your group are reluctant to share their letters with the whole group, you can: (1) share a letter you prepared ahead of time; (2) ask an adult leader to share a letter he or she prepared ahead of time; or (3) have the members of the group exchange their letters with one another.

Encourage the group members to put their letters in a safe place (such as their Bible), so that they can refer to them later. They may use them to reinforce what they believe at some time in the future or to encourage a friend who is struggling with these issues.

Optional Activity

Valuable Gifts

Hand out index cards to everyone in the group. Have them write down the possession that is most valuable to them. (It should be an object rather than a person or characteristic). Encourage them to wander around the room and find a person with whom they would trade their possession. Also, have leaders and volunteers circulate with their own cards. To make the exercise more interesting, you may want to have the leaders and volunteers carry cards with fictitious possessions, such an expensive sports car, a diamond ring, and so on.

Afterward, have the group discuss their experience. Then draw parallels between this exercise and sexual behavior. Do we treat sex like a valuable gift that we give only in special circumstances? Or do we give it away to just anybody

NOTES

for no special reason? Remind group members that how they view life and the value of sex will determine how and when they give it away.

Three

Dealing with Sexual Pressures

Objective

As a result of this lesson, students should understand that sexual behavior outside of God's boundaries carries consequences but that there is forgiveness and restoration for those who fail.

Bible Passage

Matthew 5:27-28

Materials Checklist

☐ pads of paper

☐ pens and pencils

☐ handout with sentences for "Sign Here" (optional)

Starter
(20 minutes)

Advice Column

Read the following letter aloud to your group:

Dear Gabby:

I am fifteen years old. Yesterday I found out some terrible news—I'm pregnant. My boyfriend and I knew it was wrong to have sex before marriage, but we told ourselves we couldn't help it. We thought we were careful, but I guess we weren't careful enough.

I have been numb all over since I found out. I think it will devastate my parents when I tell them. Even though they are strong Chris-

tians, I know they will be very disappointed with me. I haven't even found the nerve to tell my boyfriend. He's sixteen years old and captain of the basketball team. I don't think he's ready to be a parent.

What should I do? I'm afraid I'll have to drop out of school—I had hopes of going to college. I'm sorry for what I've done, but I don't know if I can take the shame and embarrassment of facing my friends at school and church. Maybe I should just have an abortion so that no one will ever know. I need your advice, Gabby.

Signed,

Worried Sick

Divide your group into two smaller groups. Provide each with a pad of paper and a pencil. Each group is to write a response to Worried Sick. They should address the concerns expressed in her letter. Appoint a group leader to generate discussion in each group. Also designate a group secretary to take notes for each group.

After you have given each group sufficient time to complete their assignment (10-15 minutes), have everyone rejoin the large group. Have each group's secretary read his or her group's letter. Write the group's comments and suggestions on an overhead or chalkboard. Have everyone agree on the best advice they should give Worried Sick.

Study
(15 minutes)

Say something like: **We have seen how devastating sexual behavior can be when it gets out of control. Now let's take a few minutes to see what God has to say about these issues.**

Note: Keep in mind that chapters 7, 8, and 9 cover some very important yet sensitive topics: lust, masturbation, and teen pregnancy. Even if

NOTES

a very mature group, it is likely that these topics will elicit some embarrassment and even a few snickers. It is even more likely that most, if not all, of the members of your group have never publicly discussed the topic of masturbation. As a result, you may choose to split the guys and girls into two separate groups when you discuss this topic.

1. What sights cause people to lust? (Examples: the *Sports Illustrated* swimsuit issue, love scenes in movies, tight jeans, and so on.) Next, have someone read Matthew 5:27-28. Ask: **Why did Jesus say that lusting after someone was the equivalent of adultery?**

Define lust as a burning desire for the opposite sex. Point out that the big difference between lust and love is that love always waits to give, while lust never waits to get. Jesus realized that lust is, above all, a problem of the heart. When our motives and thoughts are pure, our actions will follow.

2. What myths have you heard about masturbation? How can a young man or woman fight this temptation?

Masturbation is a common struggle. More than 60 percent of girls and more than 90 percent of guys have masturbated. Stress that it is not abnormal, but that it is wrong because: (1) it comes from lust; (2) it builds on fantasy; (3) it intensifies sensuality; (4) it focuses on pleasing self; (5) it can lead to bondage; and (6) it's second-rate sex. Review the material from *Sex: Desiring the Best* for ways of dealing with masturbation.

3. How would being pregnant or getting someone else pregnant impact the rest of a person's life?

Stress the point that teenage pregnancy has a lot of consequences that will alter a person's plans for his or her future—it will affect parents, finances, education, jobs, and friendships. You will want to make certain they know that God still loves people who get pregnant out of wedlock. Consequently, if someone is in that situation, he or she should accept God's love and forgiveness. By the same token, Christians should extend love and provide tangible help for a young man or woman who is facing an unexpected pregnancy.

Application
(15 minutes)

Provide each group member with a piece of paper and a pencil. Have each member identify silently the area he or she struggles with the most: lust, masturbation, or not loving and accepting someone he or she knows who is pregnant out of wedlock. Assure group members that their responses will be kept confidential, but allow anyone who wants to volunteer their answers.

Lust: Tell those who identified lust to write out and complete the following sentences:

(1) The thing that causes me to lust the most is (Examples: watching T.V. shows about lifeguards who run around in their bathing suits, listening to songs with explicit lyrics, and so on).

(2) The one place I go where it is most difficult to avoid lust is (Examples: the newsstand where I sneak a peek at a copy of *Playboy* magazine; Bill's house, because his dad gets *Penthouse* and leaves it lying around where we can see it).

(3) Today I will begin to get a handle on lust by committing myself to avoid (the newsstand, Bill's house). To reinforce this commitment I will ask (a friend, youth pastor, and so on) to hold me accountable to this commitment I make.

Masturbation: Tell those who identified masturbation to make a personalized action plan to deal with this problem by writing out and completing the following sentences:

(1) I want to stop masturbating because (it is a sin, God wants me to, I feel like I am a slave to it).

(2) When tempted to masturbate I will (exercise, call a friend, memorize Scripture).

(3) I will confide in (a friend, youth pastor, and so on) about my struggle with masturbation and ask him or her to hold me accountable in my effort to stop.

Teen Pregnancy: Tell those who identified loving and accepting someone who is pregnant to write out and complete the following sentences:

(1) It is a sin not to love and accept (pregnant person's name, guy's name who got her pregnant).

(2) I will show . . . (pregnant person's name, guy's name who got her pregnant), love and acceptance by . . . (telling that person I'm sorry, asking how I can help, spending time with that person, helping that person understand the options the Bible provides for him or her.)

Optional Activity

Sign Here

Write the following descriptions ahead of time on a sheet of paper. Make enough copies for each person in your group.

1. Someone who has recently read a book or watched a movie or T.V. show dealing with teenage pregnancy.

2. Someone who can name a pop song that confuses lust for love.

3. Someone who has the same color shoes as the ones you're wearing.

4. Someone who can remember to what lust was compared in the study.

5. Someone with a birthday this month.

6. Someone who can name all six of the chil-

dren from the T.V. show "The Brady Bunch."

7. Someone who can remember the four potential options for dealing with teen pregnancy from the study.

8. Someone who uses the same brand of toothpaste you use.

9. Someone who can remember the difference between lust and love.

10. Someone with the same number of brothers and sisters as you.

At the meeting give each student a copy of the above descriptions and a pencil. For each description tell them to find someone who satisfies that description's requirement. They must find a different person for each description. They must have the person who can satisfy a particular description sign his or her name next to that description. Make sure everyone understands that the person who signs next to a description must be willing to prove that he or she can satisfy the requirements of that description.

The first person to have ten valid signatures wins a prize of your choosing. Allow everyone to finish. Collect the papers of the individuals who finish first, second, and third. In front of the group, attempt to validate the signatures of the person who finished first. Ask the people who signed their name to prove that they are able to satisfy the statement next to which they signed (name the Brady children, compare shoes, etc.) If you cannot validate all ten descriptions, attempt to validate the signatures of the person who finished second. If necessary, validate the signatures of the person who finished third.

Four
Getting Control

Objective

As a result of this lesson, students should understand several key sexual problems to avoid and how to get control of their sexual behavior.

Bible Passages

1 John 1:9; 2 Timothy 2:22; 1 Corinthians 10:13

Materials Checklist

☐ two folding chairs

☐ "Straightening Out the Past" handout (see Application)

☐ sheets of poster board (optional)

☐ assortment of large markers (optional)

Starter
(20 minutes)

Critic's Corner

Ask group members to name several popular TV shows and movies that have dealt with sexual themes or in which an "alternative lifestyle" has been portrayed. Examples: an unmarried woman who chooses to have a child out of wedlock; a homosexual couple who live together; a married man who commits adultery. Note: not all of the movies or shows will necessarily have a negative content; some may deal with these topics from a Christian perspective or may show the consequences of immoral behavior.

Next, try to find two people in the group who have seen the same TV show or movie. Summon them to the front on the group and have them sit on folding chairs facing one another. Have one person defend the values shown in the movie. The other person is to criticize those values and to offer an alternative view. Encourage a humorous and lively exchange of viewpoints such as a person might see between Siskel and Ebert. Let the debate continue for a few minutes. Then choose another show or movie and a new pair of critics. Continue as time permits.

Afterward, ask your group to evaluate the arguments presented by the critics. Then ask whether such arguments have ever persuaded them to view (or stay away from) a movie or show on these subjects. Have them explain their answers.

Study
(15 minutes)

Say something like: **We have seen how the world defends its views on sexual behavior. Now let's see what God has to say about them.**

Discuss the following questions with your group:

1. Quickly address some or all of the various forms of sexual problems discussed in the book pornography, sexually transmitted diseases, homosexuality, sexual abuse, rape, and so on. Ask, According to Barry and Bill's book, how should a person deal with these sexual problems?

Review the material in chapter 10. Remind students that God can heal even the bleakest situations.

2. Have students read 1 John 1:9, 2 Timothy 2:22, and 1 Corinthians 10:13. How should these verses encourage us as we face sexual problems?

These verses assure us that we can overcome

temptations of this sort with God's help. Still, we have to make a determination to follow God's ways—it won't happen if we don't pray about it and seek His wisdom. If we fail, God grants us His forgiveness if we confess those sins.

3. What is the best way for a person to gain control over his or her sexual behavior? What should a person do if he or she has messed up in this area? What steps does a person need to take to stay out of trouble?

Most people in your group will fall into one of two categories: (1) those who have messed up sex lives they need to get under control; and (2) those who haven't gotten into trouble yet, but don't have a plan for keeping out of trouble. The first group needs a plan to get control, the second group needs a plan so they don't lose control. Share the book's four steps to gaining control: (1) realizing the need for control; (2) deciding to flee evil desires; (3) focusing on your relationship with Christ; and (4) making friends who have similar convictions.

Application
(15 minutes)

After the discussion, say something like: **I want to give you an opportunity to respond to what you have learned. Some of you need to make a commitment to straighten out your sexual behavior; others of you need to make a commitment to get control before things get out of control.**

Give each student the handout with the paragraphs/statements below written on them. Encourage each person to commit himself or herself to straightening out his or her sex life or to getting control of an area of sexual behavior before things get out of control. Because honest answers will require some vulnerability, assure group members that they may keep their answers private. Encourage them to reflect on their statements during the week.

NOTES

Straightening Out the Past

Complete the following statements:

I _____*(name)* on _____*(today's date)* commit myself to straightening out my sex life. I realize I need to renew my relationship with God, myself, and _____*(a specific person's name)*. I repent and receive God's forgiveness. I forgive myself. I will seek _____*(same person's name)* forgiveness by _____*(a specific date)*.

In order to strengthen my renewed relationship with God, I will commit myself to _____ *(suggestions: reading my Bible at least ten minutes every day, memorizing a verse a week, etc.)*. In order to reinforce the fact that I have forgiven myself, I will _____*(buy myself flowers, choose a new outfit, take myself out for a hamburger, etc.)*. Once I have asked _____*(same person's name)* for forgiveness, I will demonstrate the sincerity of my changed behavior by _____*(sending that person flowers, candy, a card, or other gift)*.

Getting Control

Read the following statements aloud, and have students complete each sentence with their own ideas.

(1) I need a plan to avoid sexual sin because (Examples: I don't want to get a sexually transmitted disease. I want to please God with my body).

(2) I am committed to staying away from (Examples: pornography, R-rated movies, the wrong types of friends) so that I don't lose control.

(3) In order to strengthen my relationship with Christ I will (Examples: read my Bible a

least five times a week, join a Bible study or discipleship group).

(4) I am committed to making new friends with similar convictions, so I will only hang around with people who (Examples: are committed to waiting till marriage to have sex, care about their relationship with Christ, will encourage me in my commitment to stay sexually pure).

Optional Activity

Purity Posters

You will need one piece of poster board and a pack of markers for every four to six people. Divide the large group into small groups of four to six each. Have each group come up with a catchy slogan that encourages sexual purity. (Examples: "Real men wait until marriage to have sex." "The only safe sex is no sex." "Give your body a break; stay sexual pure.") Have each group illustrate their message on the poster board using the markers. When all the groups have completed their posters, have each group share their poster with the rest of the group.

If you have additional time, you could have each group come up with a rap or cheer, based on their poster, that encourages sexual purity.

Part 3

LESSONS FOR
Dating:
Going Out in Style

VINCE MORRIS

Going Out in Style

An Overview in One Lesson

Objective	As a result of this study, your students will be able to summarize the main points of Barry St. Clair and Bill Jones's book *Dating: Going Out in Style*.
Bible Passages	1 Timothy 4:12; 2 Corinthians 6:14-18; Ephesians 4:31-32
Materials Checklist	☐ circle of sturdy chairs ☐ writing paper ☐ pens or pencils
Starter	**Wink 'em** Divide the group by gender. Have all the girls sit in a circle on the chairs, with one guy standing behind each girl, with his hands clasped behind his back–except for one guy, who should stand behind an empty chair. (If the ratio of guys to girls is unbalanced, have some adult leaders play, or have a mature, confident guy, or two, pretend to be a girl and take a chair!) The guy behind the empty chair tries to "get" a girl by winking; if she sees him wink at her, she should quickly slip out of her chair and run across the circle to the empty chair, leaving the

guy who lost her as the odd man out. He must wink at the other girls. The only catch is that each guy behind the girl may stop their girl from "leaving him" when he sees a wink by quickly holding his girl down in her chair by placing his hands on her shoulders (IMPORTANT: no other contact points are allowed!) before she can leave her seat.

Guys should try to hang on to their girls as long as they can, not letting those other guys steal them away with a wink. Therefore, everyone must concentrate on the winker very closely. This event is a lot of fun and very active—so make sure your chairs are sturdy! Part of the fun is watching those who can't wink very well try to "catch" a girl! To make it fair, after a few minutes switch the girls and the guys and let the girls try to "stand by their man"!

Study
(15 minutes)

1. Ask: **At what age will (or did) your parents allow you to date? Do you think an age requirement is a good idea? Why or why not?** Then have a group member read 1 Timothy 4:12. Remind students of what the authors say in chapter 2: "You are old enough to date when you are an example of what a Christian really is." Then ask: **Do you think this is too tough a limit? Why or why not?** Encourage everyone to contribute.

2. Have someone read 2 Corinthians 6:14-18 Then ask: **Based on what you read in these verses, why do you think the authors so strongly recommend against Christians dating non-Christians? What do you think is the best thing that could happen when a Christian dates a non-Christian? What is the worst?**

3. Ask: **As a Christian young man or woman, what are some of the best ways to prepare yourself for the person you may someday marry? What could you be doing**

to prepare for this person today? Tomorrow?

4. Have a person in the group read Ephesians 4:31-32. Ask: **What do these verses have to say about how a Christian should handle breaking up differently than a non-believer? How difficult is it to do what these verses say?**

Application
(15 minutes)

Mr. Postman

Give students paper, envelopes, and something to write with. Have them address the envelope to themselves. Then have everyone spend some time writing out the standards they want to have for themselves and the changes they want to make in their lives based on what they learned from *Dating: Going Out in Style*. Then have each student seal up his or her letter and turn it in to you. In a month or so, mail the letters back to them to remind them of their resolutions.

To help your group get started, you may want to hand out or read aloud the sample letter on the next page to give the students direction.

LETTER TO MYSELF

Dear _____   Date_____

I'm writing this reminder letter to myself of some of the things I learned about dating and relationships from reading *Dating: Going Out in Style*.
I have decided that God wants dating for me to be:

To pick great people to date, I intend to look for these qualities first:

About dating non-Christians, I have decided this:

To prepare myself to be an attractive date on the inside, I need to do this:

About going steady with someone, I have decided this:

If I ever need to break up with someone, I want to do it in this way:

To keep myself from sin and trouble, I have decided that these are my standards for physical contact when dating—AND I INTEND TO STICK TO THEM!

If I ever break my dating standards, I will do this right away:

And that's what I have decided about how I can serve God in my dating life!
Signed,

(Me!)

Conclude the lesson by saying: **God cares very much for each one of you and has an excellent plan for your life. If you follow His ways, you'll be happier! Enjoy your future dating life! In the meantime, I will mail these letters back to you in a few weeks to remind you of your commitment to serve God in your whole life, including your dating relationships!**

Close in prayer.

Optional Activity

Hook Tag

If you have a fairly large open area, this active game is an excellent opening mixer. Everyone needs to pair up with a partner and stand randomly around the space with their arms linked together ("hooked"). Select one person to be IT, and another person to be the pursued. IT is to chase and tag the other person. Unlike regular tag, there are no safe bases. The only way for the pursued person to avoid being caught is to hook on one of the outside arms of any of the couples standing around.

As soon as the person being chased hooks in, the person on the opposite side of the person "hooked" becomes the pursued and can be tagged by IT. If IT tags the person before he or she can link up with someone else, the tagged person becomes the new IT. (For variety, have a referee blow an occasional whistle and assign new people to be IT.) Play until you run out of time, everyone is exhausted, or you get tired of the game!

One

Understanding Dating

Objective	As a result of this study, students will understand important principles about dating and maturity that will help them make wise choices about the people they go out with.
Bible Passages	Genesis 24:57-67; 1 Timothy 4:12; Galatians 5:23, Ephesians 4:1
Materials Checklist	☐ folding or wooden chair ☐ eight role-play cards (see Application)
Starter (20 minutes)	**"Honey, If You Love Me, SMILE!"** Pick a guy and a girl who aren't too shy to begin this activity. Others will jump in as they witness the fun. Have the girl sit solemnly in a wooden or folding chair. The guy must get on his knees and look plaintively at her. He has three chances to make her smile or laugh by saying (in any pleading voice he wants), "Honey, if you love me, SMILE!" Each time he says his line, she must (without smiling at all) look directly into his eyes and say, "Honey, I love you, but I JUST CAN'T SMILE." If she can successfully keep a straight face, she switches places with him in the chair and tries to get him to smile. Otherwise, he wins, and a different girl can try her luck keeping a straight face.

Make sure everyone gets a chance to sit in the chair—this is hilarious to watch! Overacting is, of course, encouraged, and impartial judges will occasionally need to determine whether or not the "chairperson" actually did crack a smile. If you like, run this exercise as a tournament. Eliminate participants until only a "king and queen of cool" remain!

Study
(15 minutes)

Say: **Now that we've seen who are the best romancers in our group, let's learn a little about what God says about romance and dating!**

1. Have group members look up Genesis 24:57-67. Let one person read it aloud. Then ask: **How would you feel if, instead of allowing you to date, your parents chose your spouse for you?** Remind students that it still happens in many parts of the world! Have them discuss the pros and cons of this practice.

2. Ask: **At what age will (or did) your parents allow you to date? Do you think an age requirement is a good idea? Why or why not?** Then have a group member read 1 Timothy 4:12. Remind students of what the authors say in chapter 2: "You are old enough to date when you are an example of what a Christian really is." Then ask: **Do you think this is too tough a limit? Why or why not?** Encourage everyone to contribute.

3. Finally, have the group look at Galatians 5:23. Have them discuss the qualities that would be most important to them when choosing a potential date.

Application
(15 minutes)

Say: **We've spent some time exploring some ideas about romance and the spiritual side of dating. Now let's wrap things up by looking at some typical "couples" whose dating styles you may have seen before—and some you may not have seen!** Tell them to

NOTES

watch for mistakes they can avoid and lessons they can learn that will help them develop a healthier dating life.

Before the meeting, get eight pieces of poster board or cardboard. Each piece should be roughly the same size. On each piece write the name of one of the dating styles described in chapter 1 of *Dating: Going Out in Style* (dreamers, fanatics, and so on). These styles are listed below.

Choose volunteer couples (it is better to choose couples who are not dating each other) and let each take a card. Then have them act out those styles, based on how they have seen other couples behave (or perhaps on how they have acted!). Give each couple one or two minutes to play out their skit in whatever setting they think would be most appropriate for their characters. A word of caution—you may want to skip the role of "clingers," since the role-play could become embarrassing or uncomfortable for partners. At the very least, you should choose an especially mature couple to act it out.

Another variation would have the couples act out their roles on telephones. You could also let guys play girls' parts and vice versa for added humor.

Before each couple begins, introduce them by reading the descriptions listed below:

Dreamers—You are both interested in dating each other, but you just can't quite make up your mind to ask each other. So you spend lots of time stealing glances at each other, sighing, wondering how things would be between you. In fact, you even talk with each other—all about sports, school, the weather—anything but your relationship. You DO mention out loud to each other events you wouldn't mind attending, places you both enjoy, and how nice it would be to be dating someone—but somehow you can never get up the nerve to connect.

NOTES

Fanatics—You date and date and date; you never talk about anything else but dates—dates you've been on, dates you want to go on, dates other people go on. You panic at the very idea of NOT going out with someone—ANYONE! Because you are not very selective in your dating habits, as a couple you aren't very well matched at all—you have radically different interests, likes, friends, etc.—how did you ever get together, anyway?

Scooters—You are "madly in love" with each other—for now. You are always looking for the next wild romance—even while you are seeing each other, you have a "scanning eye" for the next person you want to date! As a result, you really don't spend much time on your dates getting to know each other as friends—you are looking for that next conquest or emotional high with someone else.

Squares—You have very definite ideas about how a date should go—perfect manners, the "proper" activities to go on, the "proper" way to talk with others. You are so concerned about the "right" way to date that you never loosen up and enjoy each other's friendship—you do and say everything so "formally" there's no way to discover if you might really like one another.

Lifers—You have gone together since kindergarten. You have been dating so long, you hardly know anyone else your age. Frankly, you have begun to bore each other to death—you have heard all each other's stories and jokes, but you really don't know how you would survive without your "other half." You sometimes briefly bring up seeing other people, but the thought of being "alone" in the cruel, cold world drives you back into the boring safety of each other.

Clingers—You take the physical approach to relationships. You must be in some kind of physical contact at all times, or you feel like something's wrong. You are the kind of couple

NOTES

who gross out other students in a high school hallway between classes. You have never really talked much and don't know how. You think dating is all hugs and kisses, but deep down you're not really satisfied. And sometimes you cry or are upset for "no reason."

Fighters—You just can't seem to give each other up, but all you do when you're together is fight. You are really jealous when other people "notice" or talk to your partner, and you yell at each other a lot. You break up and tearfully get back together at least once a week—sometimes more—and it seems like you can never get along together for very many minutes.

Friends—You don't really think of yourself as "an item"—you just happen to enjoy each other's friendship. You laugh a lot. You enjoy talking about your mutual relationship with Christ and how it affects your life, but that's not all you enjoy talking about by any means. You are obviously extremely comfortable and open with each other, and other people would not feel "shut off" from you just because you're together. You have become really good friends.

When everyone is finished, say: **What did you think of the various role plays? Did they accurately show what most dating styles are like? Which types seemed the healthiest? Why?**

After some student discussion, read Ephesians 4:1. Close with something like: **We've seen several different ways to approach dating in our culture. This verse talks a little about how God wants us to conduct our relationships with each other.** Remind them that God's style of dating is a growing friendship between a guy and a girl that honors Jesus Christ as each person puts the other's needs first. Tell them that over the next few weeks they'll look further into a distinctively Christian way to go about dating!

After discussion, close in prayer.

Optional Activity

Hook Tag

If you have a fairly large open area, this active game is an excellent opening mixer. Everyone needs to pair up with a partner and stand randomly around the space with their arms linked together ("hooked"). Select one person to be IT, and another person to be the pursued. IT is to chase and tag the other person. Unlike regular tag, there are no safe bases. The only way for the pursued person to avoid being caught is to hook on one of the outside arms of any of the couples standing around.

As soon as the person being chased hooks in, the person on the opposite side of the person "hooked" becomes the pursued and can be tagged by IT. If IT tags the person before he or she can link upwith someone else, the tagged person becomes the new IT. (For variety, have a referee blow an occasional whistle and assign new people to be IT.) Play until you run out of time, everyone is exhausted, or you get tired of the game!

Two

Choosing the Right Date

Objective

As a result of this study, students will learn the important connection between friendship and dating and will recognize the dangers of dating non-Christians.

Bible Passages

2 Corinthians 6:14-18; 1 Peter 3:3-4; 1 Samuel 16:7.

Materials Checklist

☐ handout with list of traits (see Starter) OR

☐ blackboard, posterboard, or newsprint

☐ index cards with one trait listed on each

☐ play money (at least $10,000 for each person present)

☐ auctioneer's gavel and stand

☐ notebook paper

☐ pens/pencils

☐ list of questions from Study section

Starter

(20 minutes)

Date Trait Auction

Provide everyone with an equal amount of play money, then auction off the various traits on the list to the highest bidder. Begin the bidding on each item (the minimum bid is listed next to each trait). Of course, when a student

NOTES

runs out of money, he or she cannot bid on anything else. Use your gavel and ring up sales— "Going once, going twice, SOLD to the young lady in the blue dress . . ."

After each sale, give the high bidder an index card with the trait they have purchased written on it. (NOTE: you may want to offer certain traits more than once so that different people have an opportunity to buy them.) After all the items have been sold off, have the students show their "purchases" and discuss who "won" the auction.

Option: make copies of the trait list, and have students check off the items they would purchase to construct their ideal date. They cannot spend more than $10,000. (Feel free to readjust the point values on the trait list if necessary before you hand it out.) If a trait they want is not on the list, they may add it—for $1,000. Afterward, have students share why they chose what they did—and what they would have purchased if they were given more money.

Date Trait List

friendly ($750)	great athlete ($800)	strong ($400)
beautiful eyes ($200)	great hair ($400)	luscious lips ($375)
bulging muscles ($200)	tender heart ($1,900)	sensitive ($850)
compassionate ($300)	great kisser ($200)	good musician ($500)
great cook ($50)	good actor ($100)	sense of humor ($1200)
outgoing ($150)	tall ($50)	gorgeous tan ($600)
great dresser ($200)	strong Christian ($3,000)	shy ($700)
loves movies ($175)	forgiving ($2,000)	peaceful ($1,400)
loves God ($2,800)	patient ($2,000)	good legs ($400)
brilliant mind ($1,800)	humble ($2,500)	rich ($2,500)

loving ($2,000)	good listener ($1,350)	good with money ($375)
good taste ($1,100)	joyful ($2,000)	happy ($1,500)
cultured ($800)	gentle ($1,900)	faithful ($2,700)
popular ($1,300)	great car ($700)	comfortable ($475)
good friend ($850)	slightly crazy ($175)	secure ($650)
nice parents ($175)	patriotic ($200)	great voice ($350)
unselfish ($2,600)	confident ($600)	other ($1000)

Study
(15 minutes)

Say: **Now that we have thought a little about what makes a great date, let's study what it means to be a great date—and what God recommends as qualities worth having in friends and dates!**

Type out or make photocopies of the following questions before the meeting. Divide into small groups (six or seven per group is ideal) to read and discuss these questions. Give one person in each group a copy of these questions and, have them lead the discussion. Same-gender groups might make conversation easier.

1. Read 2 Corinthians 6:14-18. Based on what you read in these verses, why do you think the authors so strongly recommend against Christians dating non-Christians? What do you think is the best thing that could happen when a Christian dates a non-Christian? What is the worst?

2. Dating is getting to know another person better—even if they are a member of the opposite sex! What are some of the best ways to get to know another person you're NOT dating? How would some of these methods carry over to dating life?

3. Read 1 Peter 3:3-4 and 1 Samuel 16:7. If everyone were suddenly turned inside out, so their "inner self" showed up on the outside as

their looks, what kind of person would be most attractive? Least?

Application

Say: **Based on what we learned in this study, let's find out what girls and guys REALLY want in their main squeeze!**

Divide the guys and girls into separate groups. Provide each group with paper and pens, and ask them to spend five minutes coming up with a top ten list of most important qualities their group would look for in a date. (This should be a genuine list, not just one created to draw laughs.) The entire small group should agree on these ten qualities. Then have the groups rank the qualities from one to ten, with one being the most important. When both groups are finished, have a representative from each group read the list out loud, counting down from ten to one. If possible, have someone write these traits down on a blackboard or an overhead transparency so that everyone can see the lists.

Say: **What do you think of the list the M.O.T.O.S. (members of the opposite sex) have made? Is it fair? Is it realistic? Could anyone have all ten of those characteristics?** If you have time, you may want to come up with a combined list from both groups, with the students agreeing on what is most important in a future date.

After doing this study and seeing these lists, ask each group if they would want to change their opinion of what makes a perfect date. Then ask them to think about their own dating habits and what each of them can do to make himself or herself a more attractive date. Then conclude: **Remember, God is the one you really need to impress! You are already IN a relationship with Him! He loves you no matter what and wants you to draw closer to Him. What kind of a list would you make for yourself to improve your relationship with Him?**

After discussion, close in prayer.

Optional Activity

Draw-a-Date

Make up a series of clues about dating and relationships (examples: "going steady," "date," "main squeeze," "hug," "going out," "breaking up," and so on) for a contest. Divide students into teams (guys vs. girls usually works well). Each team sends one representative to read the current word or phrase (show them only one word at a time, of course). Then both participants silently try to draw (no words, symbols, or letter hints allowed) on newsprint or a black/whiteboard a picture of the phrase so that their team can guess it first. Teams may shout out as many guesses as they like, but they may not look at the other team's drawing. The first person who correctly names the word or phrase scores for his team (you may need more than one umpire!). Keep score and rotate the "team artists" so everyone has a chance to draw.

Three

Keeping the Spark Alive

Objective	As a result of this study, students will learn how to keep dates more interested in them.
Bible Passage	Philippians 2:3-4.
Materials Checklist	☐ circle of sturdy chairs ☐ blackboard ☐ sheets of paper (shaped like Ten Commandments tablet) ☐ pens and pencils
Starter (20 minutes)	**Wink 'em** Divide the group by gender. Have all the girls sit in a circle on the chairs, with one guy standing behind each girl, with his hands clasped behind his back—except for one guy, who should stand behind an empty chair. (If the ratio of guys to girls is unbalanced, have some adult leaders play, or have a mature, confident guy, or two, pretend to be a girl and take a chair!) The guy behind the empty chair tries to "get" a girl by winking; if she sees him wink at her, she should quickly slip out of her chair and run across the circle to the empty chair, leaving the guy who lost her as the odd man out. He must

wink at the other girls. The only catch is that the guys behind the girls may stop their girls from "leaving them" when they see a wink by quickly holding their girl down in her chair by placing his hands on her shoulders (IMPORTANT: no other contact points are allowed!) before she can leave her seat.

Guys should try to hang on to their girls as long as they can, not letting those other guys steal them away with a wink. Therefore, everyone must concentrate on the winker very closely. This event is a lot of fun and very active—so make sure your chairs are sturdy! Part of the fun is watching those who can't wink very well try to "catch" a girl! To make it fair, after a few minutes switch the girls and the guys and let the girls try to "stand by their man"!

Study
(15 minutes)

Say something like: **Well, now we know who is really good at hanging on to a man or woman! Now let's learn what it takes to do that in real life!**

Before the meeting, type out or photocopy the following questions. Divide into small groups (six or seven per group) to read and discuss the following questions. Give a copy of the questions to one person in each group; he or she will lead the discussion. Same-gender groups might make conversation easier.

1. Of all the date ideas Bill and Barry listed in chapter 7, which ones appealed the most to you? the least? Why?

2. As a Christian young man or woman, what are some of the best ways to prepare yourself for the person you may someday marry? What could you be doing to prepare for this person today? Tomorrow?

3. Read Philippians 2:3-4. What makes a humble, caring person easier to be around than a conceited, selfish one? How could these verses apply to your dating and friendships?

86

Application
(15 minutes)

Say: **There are many ways to make yourself and your planned dating time more interesting—but there are also many ways to blow it. There ARE certain rules for dating that will help you have a better experience: "Thou shalt not pick thy nose in public,"** for instance, and **"Thou shalt listen to thy date occasionally instead of talking about thyself all night." Let's see if we can come up with The Ten Greatest Commandments for Relationships.**

Pass out sheets of paper (if you have time, cut the paper to resemble the tablets of the Ten Commandments), pens, and pencils. Encourage students to suggest both funny and serious relationship rules for how to be a good servant of God, a good friend, and a good date. Discourage the crude and rude, and write down the good suggestions on the board.

When students have listed several simple rules, distribute sheets of paper and have them list the top ten most important rules for them to remember personally from the longer list posted up front. Each person will experience different trouble spots in his or her relationships, so this exercise should be a personal one that allows students to be honest with themselves. Still, encourage those who are willing to share their list with the group.

After the meeting, have the students take their Ten Commandments home with them to post on their bedroom wall or to use as bookmarks to remind them of these important areas for improvement.

Remind students that creative dating is a lot of work. Preparation pays off, whether you are creating a date that is fun and interesting, getting ready for the date, or especially preparing yourself to date someone, someday, somewhere. Conclude by saying something like: **Don't forget that the most important way to make** yourself interesting is to focus on other people. In Mark 9:35 Jesus says, "If anyone wants to be first, he must be the very last, and the servant of all." When you live that way, you'll have no problem keeping dates interested in you! Even better, you will be living as Christ wants us all to live, and there's nothing uninteresting about that!"

Close the meeting in prayer.

Optional Activity

Oldlywed Game

Invite three or four long-married couples (who don't mind potential mild embarrassment!) from your church or neighborhood to participate in an "Oldlywed Game," in which they answer questions from a game-show host (better if the host can be a distinguished, tuxedoed smooth-talker) about each other and their marriage.

Divide the contest into several rounds, as time permits. Each successive question should be worth more points than the previous one (and should be more difficult to answer!). For the first round, send the husbands to a separate room. Then ask the first question. The wives are to tell the audience (your students) how their spouse would answer the questions being asked. (Have someone write down their responses.) Ask three to five questions per round, then bring in the spouses, who then are asked the same questions. For the next round, send the wives to the separate room and have the husbands answer the questions.

Make up your own questions ahead of time, based on what you know about your participants. Typical questions might be "How many times a year does your spouse give you flowers?" "What is the most creative date you and your spouse have ever gone on together?" "How many times did you and your spouse break up before you finally married?" "What is the last movie you

NOTES

BOTH really enjoyed together?" "What is your spouse's favorite food?" and so on.

Keep score (you may even want to videotape this event for posterity), and reward the participants with gift certificates to a nice restaurant. Vary the quality of the restaurant depending on their performance in the game (first place—nice restaurant; second place—OK restaurant; third—fast-food restaurant).

Four

Going beyond Casual Dating

Objective	As a result of this study, students will learn how to handle the ups and downs of dating.
Bible Passages	Romans 12:1-2; Ephesians 4:31-32
Materials Checklist	☐ notebook paper ☐ pencils/pens ☐ large sheet of newsprint OR several smaller squares of paper

Starter
(20 minutes)

Spectragraph

Place a long sheet of newsprint on the floor or on the wall, designed to look like a scale from minus 10 to plus 10 like this:

Disagree   Neutral   Agree
10–9–8–7–6–5–4–3–2–1–0–1–2–3–4–5–6–7–8–9–10

Note: You may also write each number on a smaller sheet of paper and tape these numbers to the floor.

Ask the students to respond to some of the statements below. They are to answer by taking their place along the Spectragraph, one person per number. (You may want to have everyone remove their shoes if they stand on the paper!)

NO MORE THAN THREE people can occupy any single number at one time; if more want to answer that way, they must explain why they should have the right to stand on the spot. The group must decide on the three people who can make the strongest case for their choices. Those three can stay, while the other people must find new numbers. You will learn a lot about each other's opinions on the subjects! (Feel free to add your own questions to make the lesson more flexible and adapt it to your specific group.)

Sample Spectragraph statements:

1. Dating one person steadily is always a bad idea for high schoolers.

2. You should never date anyone your parents do not fully approve of.

3. God thinks dating in general is a bad idea.

4. The typical busy high schooler shouldn't date more than twice a month.

5. Even people who are dating steadily shouldn't kiss for at least 3 months.

6. A person shouldn't ever date anyone over 20 years older than he or she is.

7. A guy should always bring a present or flowers on the first date.

8. There really isn't any difference between dating and spending time with a friend.

9. One of the best places to meet future dates is at church events.

10. Girls shouldn't be allowed to ask guys out on a date.

Study
(15 minutes)

Say: **Now that we've gotten to know each other a little better, let's get into the nitty gritty of long-term dating relationship and their ups and downs.**

Before the meeting, type out or photocop the following questions. Divide into smal groups (six to seven per group) to read and discuss the following questions. Give one copy of the questions to a leader of your choosing for each group. Same-gender groups might make conversation easier.

1. What kinds of security do some people seek in a dating relationship? If people need security in their lives, why would a committed dating relationship be a bad place to get it? When would it be OK?

2. Have a person in the group read Ephesians 4:31-32. What do these verses have to say about how a Christian should handle breaking up differently than a nonbeliever? How difficult is it to do what these verses say?

3. Look up Romans 12:1-2 and have one person read it aloud. If Christians are to present their bodies to God, is anyone else entitled to them? What level of physical contact is OK in a dating relationship?

Application
(15 minutes)

Declaration of Dependence

Say: **Setting personal standards of purity is perhaps the single most important issue for you to resolve before it becomes an issue. It's too late to go out to buy fire extinguishers when the carpet is on fire! In fact, one of the biggest reasons people who have been going together have problems and break up is because they never agreed on standards they could stick with. Let's spend some time right now buying fire extinguishers for our future (and present!) relationships!**

Give each student a piece of paper and a pen or pencil; have them write down some important standards for physical contact and involvement that they intend to keep when they date. Everyone can begin their paper with "I hereby highly resolve . . ." or some other official language (you could even hand out sheets of paper

93

NOTES

with those words printed or written in a fancy script on them). Have everyone sign and date their copy. If possible, have one or two people sign each paper as "official witnesses" who pledge to help hold the signer accountable to his or her pledge. Have the students take the paper home to remind them of their relationship priorities. (If you like, hand out some form of the sample document below to give the students a general outline for their documents.)

Declaration of Dependence
(on God for Personal Purity)

On this, the _____ day of _____, 19_____, in order to maintain good relationships with current or future dates, to stay free of physical and mental disease and trauma, and to keep my conscience pure before God, I hereby highly resolve to establish these preventative standards concerning my physical relationship with the opposite sex:

1 I will avoid compromising situations by:

2 I will establish these as my physical lines in dating, which I will NOT cross under any circumstances:

3 If I am tempted or fail in this resolve I will immediately take these steps to correct the situation:

4 In addition, I pledge myself to the following:

I do hereby establish this document as a permanent pledge and memorial to my desire to honor God in my physical being, as well as with the rest of my life. May the witness(es) below hold me accountable to it and to God.

Signature: _____

Witnesses: _____

Say: **By now we have talked about almost every aspect of relationships with the op-**

posite sex that there is! Remember—God can heal broken relationships—but if you put some of the principles in practice that we've talked about in these lessons, you will be better prepared to have WONDER-FUL relationships for the rest of your life!

Close the meeting in prayer.

Optional Activity

Place-Your-Pucker Contest

Divide into guys' and girls' teams. Get posters or blown-up photos of movie stars or famous personalities (option: use photos of some good-natured group members who can take a joke) and post them at head-level on the wall. Apply a cheap tube of bright red lipstick to everyone's lips (even the guys'!). Blindfold everyone one at a time and have a place-your-pucker contest (like pin-the-tail-on-the-donkey) to see who can kiss the picture closest to the real mouth!